WATER

S E Y M O U R   S I M O N

Peachtree

HARPER
An Imprint of HarperCollinsPublishers

*To water scientists who help us understand
our planet Earth*

Special thanks to Robert Byrne

PHOTO AND ART CREDITS: Page 2: © Hdsidesign/Dreamstime.com; page 4: © NASA (Image by Robert Simmon and Marit Jentoft-Nilsen, based on MODIS data); page 7: © Doug Allan/Nature Picture Library; page 8: © Nigel Cattlin/Science Source; pages 10–11: © Liz Nealon; page 13: © isarescheewin/Shutterstock; page 14: © Sergey Ryzhov/Shutterstock; page 17: Water cycle diagram courtesy of the National Weather Service/National Oceanic and Atmospheric Administration; page 18: © Benny Marty/Shutterstock; page 21: © Sven Zacek/Nature Picture Library; page 22: © Jerry Monkman/Nature Picture Library; page 25: © Floris van Breugel/Nature Picture Library; pages 26–27: © Phil Degginger /Science Source; page 29: © f9photos/Shutterstock; page 30: © Abramov Timur/Shutterstock; page 33: © Georgette Douwma /Science Source; page 34: © Manan Vatsyayana/Getty Images; page 37: © James Cavallini /Science Source; pages 38–39: © Jackbluee/ Dreamstime.com

Library of Congress Control Number: 2017932846
ISBN 978-0-06-247055-3 (trade bdg.) — ISBN 978-0-06-247054-6 (pbk.)

17 18 19 20 21 SCP 10 9 8 7 6 5 4 3 2 1

❖
First Edition

Author's Note

From a young age, I was interested in animals, space, my surroundings—all the natural sciences. When I was a teenager, I became the president of a nationwide junior astronomy club with a thousand members. After college, I became a classroom teacher for nearly twenty-five years while also writing articles and books for children on science and nature even before I became a full-time writer. My experience as a teacher gives me the ability to understand how to reach my young readers and get them interested in the world around us.

I've written more than 300 books, and I've thought a lot about different ways to encourage interest in the natural world, as well as how to show the joys of nonfiction. When I write, I use comparisons to help explain unfamiliar ideas, complex concepts, and impossibly large numbers. I try to engage your senses and imagination to set the scene and to make science fun. For example, in *Penguins*, I emphasize the playful nature of these creatures on the very first page by mentioning how penguins excel at swimming and diving. I use strong verbs to enhance understanding. I make use of descriptive detail and ask questions that anticipate what you may be thinking (sometimes right at the start of the book).

Many of my books are photo-essays, which use extraordinary photographs to amplify and expand the text, creating different and engaging ways of exploring nonfiction. You'll also find a glossary, an index, and website and research recommendations in most of my books, which make them ideal for enhancing your reading and learning experience. As William Blake wrote in his poem, I want my readers "to see a world in a grain of sand, / And a heaven in a wild flower, / Hold infinity in the palm of your hand, / And eternity in an hour."

Seymour Simon

Water is a natural substance and is important for our planet in many ways. For instance, water is the most common liquid on Earth. Because of the temperatures found on much of the surface of our planet, water is usually in liquid form. Water helps regulate Earth's temperature, keeping it just right for living things—neither too hot nor too cold.

Not only is water important to our planet, but it is also crucial for people. Water regulates the temperature of the human body, carries nutrients and **oxygen** to cells in the body, removes wastes, and protects organs and tissues. Our bodies are mostly made of water. A person might be able to live for a month without food but could only survive for about a week without water.

There is about the same amount of water on Earth now as when Earth was first formed. The glass of water you drink today might contain **molecules** of water that a dinosaur drank millions of years ago. Without water, our planet would be a lifeless ball of rock tumbling through space, more like the moon than the active blue orb we call Earth. Perhaps planet Earth should have been named planet Water.

A molecule of water, H_2O, contains two **atoms** of **hydrogen** and one atom of oxygen. Water is a mass of water molecules held together by electrical attractions. Water is the only substance on Earth that is found naturally in all three states of matter: as a liquid (water), as a solid (ice), and as a gas (water **vapor**).

Water changes from a liquid form to solid ice at 32° Fahrenheit (0° Celsius). When water freezes, the molecules lock together in an interconnected pattern of molecules that form ice crystals. The molecules of ice are farther apart than the molecules of liquid water, which makes ice lighter than water. As a result, ice floats, which means that ponds, lakes, and oceans freeze from the top down, not from the bottom up. Because of that simple but important fact, living things can survive in cold weather because most bodies of water do not freeze into a solid chunk of ice, and liquid water remains at the bottom even in the coldest winter.

When water is heated, its molecules move faster and faster. At sea level, the boiling point of water is 212°F (100°C). When molecules move faster, they may break free and fly into the air as an invisible gas called water vapor. Water absorbs a lot of heat before it boils. That's why water is used in car radiators to cool the hot engine.

Despite being made up of only two of the very lightest elements, hydrogen and oxygen, water is heavy. That's because water molecules are tightly attracted to each other and close together. Since water is very dense, many less dense substances, such as wood and oil, float on water.

Where the water meets the air on the surface of a body of water, water molecules cling very closely to one another. The elastic film of surface water molecules at the water-air boundary is called surface tension. Surface tension is strong enough to support the weight of water striders and some other insects, small spiders, birds, and reptiles.

In the air, water molecules also come together to form small, ball-shaped raindrops. Rain that lands on glass windows and house shingles spreads out into a thin layer. But if rain lands on surfaces that repel water, such as the smooth metals of automobiles and some kinds of plant leaves, the rainwater pulls together again into a ball shape.

Water is called the "universal solvent" because it dissolves more substances than any other liquid. Even rocks are dissolved by water, though it may take many years. You can see this if you look at rock tombstones in a cemetery. The inscriptions on old tombstones are often hard to read because of rain that has fallen over centuries, weathering the rock.

Natural water is almost never pure. Earth's surface contains many minerals and other substances that have been dissolved in the water. Ocean water is salty because it is full of dissolved minerals. Water can also carry along particles of sand and mud that don't dissolve easily, as seen in the muddy water in a river or lake. This kind of water is called a suspension. Because water is such an excellent solvent, it can carry lots of minerals and other dissolved substances. Soil filters water in underground wells and **aquifers** (underground layers of rock saturated with water). Yet chemicals and gases dissolved in water can still cause problems. Water can also carry germs and viruses that cause disease.

Pure water is neither acidic nor basic, so we say it has a neutral **pH** of 7. Depending on what is dissolved in the water, the pH level changes. Acids have a lower pH and bases have a higher pH. Most pH values are from 1 to 14. Ocean water is usually basic with a pH between 7.5 and 8.5. Ammonia is a strong base, with a pH of about 11. Soda is an acid with a pH of about 4. Vinegar, even more acidic, has a pH of about 2.4. Acidic foods, such as pickles, taste sour. Bases, such as baking soda, have a bitter flavor.

Water is the main substance in our bodies. Almost two-thirds of an adult's weight is water and nearly 80 percent of a newborn baby's weight is water. Losing even 10 percent of the water in our bodies can make us seriously ill. Even though a person can survive without food for nearly a month, a person without water can only survive several days. Here are a few reasons why water is so important to our bodies:

- Water is a vital nutrient in the life of every cell of our bodies. Water is needed to build new cells and keep old cells alive.
- The proteins and carbohydrates in food that our bodies need are carried by the water in our bloodstreams.
- Water regulates our internal body temperature through sweating.
- Water forms saliva, which helps digest food in our mouths. It also flushes wastes from the body through the kidneys.
- Water acts as a shock absorber for the brain, the spinal cord, and for an unborn fetus.

Without water there would be no you and me. There wouldn't be any people, any animals, or any plants—no living things on Earth at all—without water.

Water is always on the move, constantly changing to and from water vapor, liquid water, and ice. This is called the water cycle. One way to visualize it is to follow a drop of water on its journey. We can begin anywhere, but let's begin in the ocean. Heat from the sun warms the surface of the ocean and our drop of water evaporates, becoming water vapor and rising higher and higher into the air. Strong winds grab the drop and carry it for miles until it is over land.

Warm updrafts from sun-warmed lands push the drop still higher into the atmosphere, where the air is cold. When the drop cools enough, it condenses back into a liquid. If it is very cold, it might turn into a tiny ice crystal and become part of an icy cirrus cloud. But our drop cools into a drop of liquid water that forms around a tiny speck of dust or smoke or a salt crystal to become part of a cumulus or stratus rain cloud.

The drop combines with millions of others to fall as rain. If the atmosphere is cold enough, the drop might fall as snow or sleet. Perhaps the drop lands on a patch of soil, a plant leaf, or a street. It might evaporate again, or it might sink into the soil and finally join together to become part of an underground aquifer and then part of a stream or a river. The journey could take many years, but finally the drop will return to an ocean or other body of water, continuing its endless travels through the water cycle.

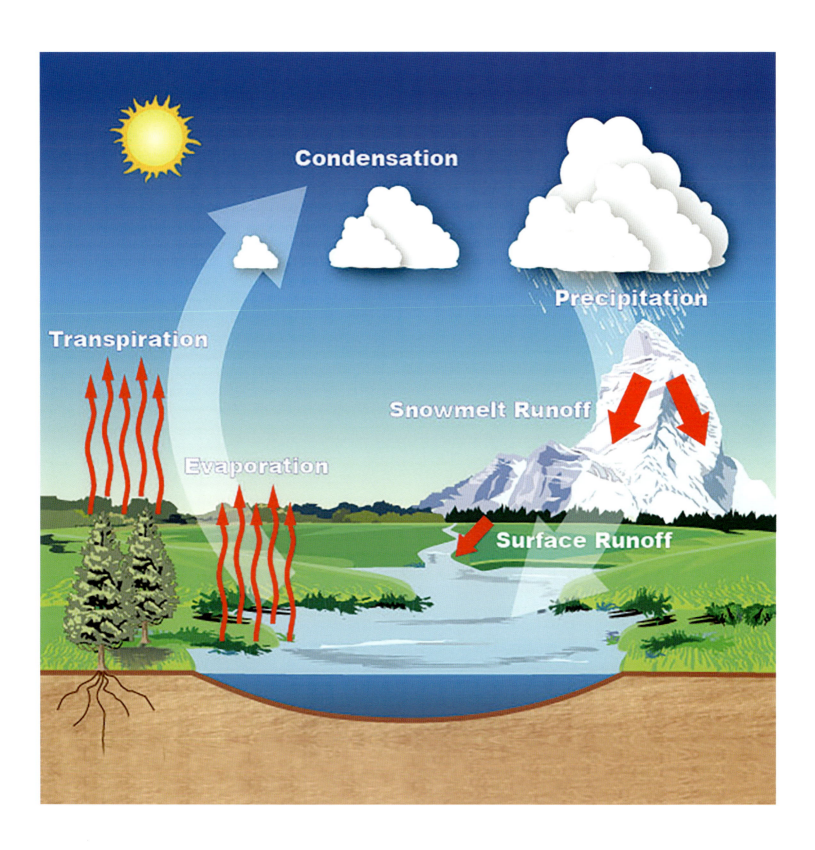

The water cycle describes how water is continually moving through Earth's ground, surface, and atmosphere. But a majority of Earth's water is not constantly on the move in the water cycle and instead remains in storage in the oceans. All of Earth's water is estimated to be about 332 million cubic miles (1,386 million cubic kilometers) and 96.5 percent of that can be found in the oceans. For all the tens of millions of cubic miles of water moving through the water cycle, there is nearly twenty times more water stored in the oceans. Through **evaporation** the oceans also supply about 90 percent of the water that goes into the water cycle.

Over tens or even hundreds of years, the amount of water in the oceans doesn't change by much. But over many thousands of years, the level of the oceans does change. During the last Ice Age, twenty thousand years ago, when the climate was much colder, the ocean levels were three feet (one meter) lower than they are today. The reason is because so much of the ocean water was locked up as ice.

The reverse is true during warmer stretches like now, which is a result of global warming. The ocean levels rise as the ice melts. During the last global warm spell about 125,000 years ago, the ocean levels were about 18 feet (5.5 meters) higher than during the Ice Age. Scientists believe that current global warming will result in a similar rise in ocean waters. That means that coastal cities will have to deal with flooding as the ocean levels rise.

Currently more than two-thirds of the freshwater on Earth is frozen in glaciers and ice sheets. Only about 30 percent of freshwater is in the ground and in lakes and rivers. Water that falls as rain, snow, or other forms of **precipitation** may fall directly on lakes, ponds, or rivers. But most precipitation lands on the ground. Once on the ground, it might sink into the soil as groundwater or journey down into an underground storage place within the soil called an aquifer.

Some of the water in the ground might be pumped up to the surface and used for drinking, washing, sanitation, or irrigation for crops. Some of the water might form underground streams that come to the surface and join with other streams in a larger river. Particles of soil are carved out of the ground by the running water and carried along to lower places.

Over thousands of years, rivers carve out valleys and shape the ground. The rivers may form lakes. Water from lakes may join rivers and flow back to the oceans or evaporate back into the air. Maybe the water will be stored in water tanks or used to fight fires, tend a garden, or flush a toilet. People need water for almost everything. The possibilities are endless.

Water exists as ice in below-freezing temperatures in many places around the world. The upper slopes and tops of higher mountains are cold and covered by ice and snow all year round. The Antarctic continent is covered by miles-thick layers of ice and snow that never melt. Parts of Alaska, Canada, Greenland, and Iceland are also covered by frozen water throughout the year. Summertime fields of ice and snow also exist in the Rocky Mountains of the United States, the Alps of Europe, the Himalayas of Asia, the Andes of South America, and even high atop Mount Kilimanjaro at the equator in Africa.

Even during the warmer months of summer, ice and snow cover about one-tenth of Earth's surface. These high regions of everlasting snow are said to be above the snow line, where there is snow on the ground even during the summer.

Glaciers are born above the snow line. They sometimes form when snowfields do not melt in the summer. The snow turns to ice and becomes thicker and thicker. As years go by, the mass of ice begins to slide downhill. When an ice field begins to move, it becomes a river of ice, a glacier. Ice moves differently than water. Water flows easily and quickly. The glaciers move slowly, sometimes only an inch or two a day.

Deserts are dry areas that occupy about one-third of Earth's land surface. However, not all deserts are full of sand. Polar deserts can be found in the Arctic and Antarctic. But most deserts are above freezing for at least part of the year. What they have in common is that their rainfall (or snowfall) is less than ten inches a year and in some places a lot less. Few living things can survive in the cold of the Antarctic or Arctic snowfields.

In contrast to deserts, rainforests are the wettest places in the world. A rainforest gets at least sixty inches of rain a year. Only about 2 percent of Earth's surface is rainforests, but they are home to millions of animals (mostly insects) and plants. Living things get all the water they need in a rainforest.

Rain and snow are forms of precipitation, the main way that water in the sky comes down to Earth's surface. Precipitation fills lakes and rivers, underground aquifers, reservoirs, oceans, and seas. The amount of precipitation that falls around the world ranges from less than an inch a year in some deserts to an average of more than 450 inches a year on Mount Waialeale in Hawaii.

What happens to the water when it reaches the ground depends upon how fast it falls, the soil conditions, the plant density, the temperature, and where it falls, whether in a city or the countryside. Direct **runoff** in a city to a river, lake, or ocean occurs very quickly. That's because roofs and paved streets permit less rain to soak into the ground. Storm sewer systems carry the water directly to a nearby body of water. Precipitation in a natural, undeveloped area goes much more slowly into rivers and lakes.

In the United States, about 70 percent of yearly precipitation returns to the atmosphere by evaporation from land and water and by **transpiration** (when plants give off water vapor through pores in their leaves). The remaining 30 percent finally reaches a stream, river, lake, or ocean by runoff or by moving through the ground.

Water is much denser and heavier than air. The deeper the water, the greater the weight of water pressing from above. This is called water pressure. The weight of the air, or air pressure, at sea level is about 14.7 pounds per square inch. Water pressure increases one atmosphere (about 14.7 pounds per square inch) for every 33 feet (10 meters) of water depth. Most scuba divers don't go deeper than about 250 feet down, where the pressure is eight and a half times greater than at the surface. They could lose consciousness below that. But the average depth of the oceans is about two and a half miles. Down there, the water pressure is about 3 tons per square inch. That means that deep-sea submersibles need thick walls made of very strong materials to prevent them from being crushed.

Sound waves travel about four times faster in water than they do in air. The sounds also travel much farther in water. A whale's song, for example, can be heard by another whale many miles away. That's also why sound detection devices such as sonar can pick up the sounds of ships from far away.

Light rays are also absorbed by water. Most sunlight is gone at depths below 1,000 feet. Light is composed of all the colors in a rainbow. Blue light penetrates more deeply than the other colors. So at depths below 500 feet, the ocean waters appear blue. At depths below 3,000 feet (900 meters), there is no sunlight at all, and the water is dark. Yet even at the bottom of the sea, some kinds of life exist in the dark, dense waters. In fact, life exists in any watery place on Earth that is not polluted.

Water is a precious resource for the people and other living things on Earth. But people need water that does not contain harmful chemicals or pollutants. In some communities, such as Flint, Michigan, and for hundreds of millions of people living in developing countries around the world, safe drinking water is not easily available. Poverty, wars, and natural disasters make dirty, unfiltered water a major health problem in the world.

Here are some facts about water:

- Depending upon weight, a healthy person needs to take in about 2 to 3 quarts of water a day.

- Of all the freshwater on Earth, about 75 percent is stored in polar ice and glaciers and about 25 percent is stored in aquifers underground. Less than 1 percent is in rivers and lakes and in soil. Yet most of the water we drink comes from surface waters.

- The average amount of water used by each person in the United States is about 80 to 100 gallons of water every day. The largest use of water in the home is to flush toilets and, after that, to take showers and baths.

- It takes about 2 to 4 gallons of water to flush a toilet. It takes about 70 gallons to fill a bathtub and about 35 gallons to take a shower.

- A leaky faucet or toilet can waste 100 gallons of water in a day. Brushing your teeth and washing the dishes with an open faucet the entire time wastes tens of gallons of water each time.

Most of the world's cities and towns are located near sources of freshwater. People have used water not only to drink and grow crops, but they have also built ships to travel on rivers, lakes, and over the ocean for discovery and trade. More than any other substance, water is part of our history and part of our existence.

Water is almost everywhere on Earth—in the air and the clouds; on the surface in oceans, lakes, rivers, and ice; in plants and animals; and inside Earth in the top few miles of ground. But when water supplies are contaminated for one reason or another, people are in harm's way. Water is an essential part of life as we know it. When we look to find life on distant planets or moons, the first thing we look for is water.

GLOSSARY

Aquifer—An underground layer of water-permeable rock, sand, or gravel. Aquifers are huge storages of water on our planet.

Atom—The smallest particle of an element that still has the properties of that element.

Condensation—The act or process by which a gas, such as water vapor, cools and changes into a liquid, such as water.

Evaporation—The change from a liquid into a gas.

Hydrogen—A nonmetallic element that is the simplest and lightest of the elements.

Molecule—The smallest particle of an element or compound that retains all the properties of that substance. Molecules are made up of two or more atoms linked by chemical bonds.

Oxygen—A gaseous element that makes up about one fifth of Earth's atmosphere and is colorless, odorless, and tasteless.

pH—A measure of acidity and alkalinity of a solution that is a number on a scale ranging from 0, the most acid, to 14, the most alkaline. Pure water has a value of 7, which is neutral.

Precipitation—The process by which water vapor in the atmosphere cools and turns into water or ice in the form of rain, snow, hail, or sleet.

Runoff—Water from rain or snow that flows over land usually into streams and rivers.

Transpiration—The passage of water from a plant into the atmosphere as water vapor.

Vapor—A gas from a substance that is usually a liquid at room temperature. Water vapor is water in its gaseous state.

INDEX

READ MORE ABOUT IT

Seymour Simon's website
www.seymoursimon.com

EPA Water Sense Kids
wwww.epa.gov/watersense/watersense-kids

Water Education Foundation
www.watereducation.org/water-kids

U.S. Geological Survey
www2.usgs.gov/water

Water Use It Wisely
wateruseitwisely.com/kids